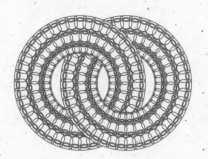

SCRAPING AWAY

Scraping Away

Fred Shaw

CAVANKERRY
PRESS

CavanKerry Press Ltd.
Fort Lee, New Jersey
www.cavankerrypress.org

Publisher's Cataloging-In-Publication Data
(Prepared by The Donohue Group, Inc.)
Names: Shaw, Fred, 1972- author.
Title: Scraping away / Fred Shaw.
Description: First edition. | Fort Lee, New Jersey : CavanKerry Press, 2020.
Identifiers: ISBN 9781933880785
Subjects: LCSH: Restaurants—Employees—Poetry. | Restaurants—Employees—
     Family relationships—Poetry. | Working class—Poetry. | LCGFT: Poetry.
Classification: LCC PS3619.H3932 S37 2020 | DDC 811/.6—dc23

Cover and interior text design by Mayfly Design
First Edition 2020, Printed in the United States of America

CavanKerry Press is grateful for the support it receives from the New Jersey State Council on the Arts.

ALSO BY FRED SHAW

Argot (2014)

*This book is dedicated to all those who know
what it takes to make a shift go smooth.*

*And to Kristina, who keeps me centered
with her love and laughter.*

CONTENTS

III

FOREWORD

In his celebration of the writer Theodor Storm, James Wright says that "Storm understood that the main thing was not to make a successful career, but to live one's life. . . . that the main thing is not to get on in the world but to get home." I think the poems in *Scraping Away* are saying something like that, confronting the difficulties which working-class life intensifies—marginality, failure, economic fragility—and affirming what sustains us in the face of them—love, music, the achievement of a communal tongue. Recognizing the difficulties is why Shaw's affirmations matter, why in spite of everything "work / can be worship."

Shaw's is a decidedly blue-collar world full of "the smells of grease / and rust," abandoned mills and warehouses, an inherited toolbox, a world which inevitably involves us with the death of friends and loved ones and the waking death of the eight-hour shift, of that coming-of-age violence where desire's the hunger for whatever flesh can be held against one's own, all soundtracked by music, mostly jazz, including a stint in New Orleans where it feels as if the funeral has just stormed past, rinsing the air, the initials left "in the Quarter's wet cement" another testament, like the poem's, of a singular human presence.

That the crucible of labor here is mostly restaurant work allows Shaw to make clear if understated connections among kinds of hunger and matters of the tongue, between food and language, the kitchen serving as a connection between home and workplace, private and public worlds. In the poem "Argot" we're told of "a working life / that takes what it wants, stealing my pen." In "The Paper Signs" language is wholly appropriated by the boss, her nearly Mosaic list of prohibitions (*"Keep your mouths shut"*) posted just inside the door. We're in a world whose pleasures are meant for someone else ("delivering dumb calories / to hungry mouths"). Set corrective to all of this is the kitchen table the poet remembers in "The Place Setting":

> On it, three generations of women
>
> have rolled *kluski*, powdering
> pressed-out stretches with flour.

No alienation from labor here, where the ties between language and nourishment, both spiritual and physical, have been lovingly established.

Such privileged moments reveal themselves whenever "something alive and escaped" shines through the routine welter of the daily grind. It's there when his exuberant father, back from the bar, conducts "an invisible orchestra" playing Beethoven's Sixth, in the "dusty summer note" he manages from a writing class, or when he and a friend "blow off / jive-ass jobs" to pound out rhythms in a city park, using broken branches in a joyous imitation of "Blakey chopping wood."

For me the most notable of these moments takes place in the title poem when a dropped plate of scallops affords the work staff, after "scraping away the broken to save the unscathed," the luxury of eating them, some for the first time. In its seemingly offhand recounting of an incident at work, the poem explores class and labor, profit and loss, the behind-the-scenes reality which privilege ignores and on which it depends, the poet proceeding the way Giacometti did, getting to the essence of an experience by working through what surrounds it, shucking the this-and-that to get to the gist, and revealing in the process "the far-off places of ourselves" which, paradoxically, are shown to be ever close at hand.

In this, as well as in its wealth of detail from a world that's palette to the physical senses, *Scraping Away* is reminiscent of Studs Terkel's great book of oral history, *Working*, its kindred firsthand testaments of blue-collar life now passed through the alembic into poetry.

—Robert Gibb, author of *After*,
winner of the Marsh Hawk Press Poetry Prize

i.

*Jaws clenched tight we talked all night
oh but what the hell did we say?
The good times are killing me.*

—Modest Mouse

Argot

In the sweaty restaurant kitchen,
where I'll learn to cuss in Mexican,
tattooed line cooks talk shit in voices
nicked as the bone-white
monkey bowls we stack and fill.

They call the boss and picky customers
chupacabra, "goat sucker,"
being the inside joke
for every pain in the ass.

Years ago, in a place once a mustard factory,
I was a boy touring Mom's latest food-prep gig,
a windowless world where the clam chowder
paddled around in vats
deep enough for me to stand,

and I wore a paper hat,
same as the mustached men in bloody aprons
who cut up and kidded while they hacksawed
T-bones from beef sides.

Now, I'm digging twelve-hour grooves
of full trays in spaghetti joints
with family names. I'm keeping ice bins full
and counters clean, wondering, at times,

if the routine has replaced the oxygen
of my dreams with a working life
that takes what it wants, stealing my pen
and handing me
bad math on credit slips.

On her days off,
Mom wants to play Scrabble,
but instead, we talk about our fingers,
how they've split into open-flowered nerves,
stinging our bodies to the bulk

of a weary self at the end of the day,
each of us searching
for the phrase that captures what it is
to feel at once,
both capable and small.

Curse

Waiting for steak and fries
beneath this dining room's cold light, I look on
as Angelita, the stocky Paiute waitress, hauls
ales and elk burgers to tables of Germans
touring Utah parks on Beemer bikes.

It took until senior year for me to balance
a full tray of steaming chow, elbow wobbling
until I learned to spread fingers wide, hoisting
the fiberglass oval on the level plain
of my palm, held steady above my right shoulder.

And when the boss said to hustle, I wore
a ready smile and worked without pause, buffing
lipstick from wine glass rims, scooping up
what was left behind—spoons and mugs half-full of cold coffee,
chicken bones and change, once a slimy denture.

Delivering dumb calories
to hungry mouths is enough to consider
the flocks of fried fowl,
the braised and broiled herds I've lugged,
three plates at a time

on one of my skinny limbs,
and to wonder if it's worth sharing
with this hardworking woman
how I measured out my tired body by the decade,
one arm grown longer than the other.

José at the Yum-Yum Café

stir-fries a blistering wok of lo mein,
an illegal cooking this Szechuan dish
for sweatshirted undergrads who slurp
their noodles through chopsticks while he works
over blue-flamed burners in a steamy kitchen,
the steady heat of gas stoves like a rippled
current of manual days and long labor.

Over a joint at my girl's apartment he recounts
his journey, pausing to find the right phrases.
From a Costa Rican village to border crossing,
for a thousand dollars he was smuggled
in the back of an aluminum U-Haul. José landscaped
beneath a heavy-handed Houston sun, then scrubbed
dishes in a hundred Chicago eateries before coming
to Pittsburgh's gray shore of opportunity.

Maybe his America is now a cold-blooded embrace
or a soggy foot, maybe it's a wink,
a paycheck under the table,
tenement rent deducted from a nonnegotiable wage,
one nation united in its willingness to give him
a bite, if only it can take its own bite back.

Before I move to New Orleans, José asks me for help
with his broken English. He wants to enroll in college.
My time short, I give him a book of poems,
Bukowski lifted from a bookstore in my baggy pants,
thinking that it'll be a helpful and amusing way
to learn the syntax of broken promises
and understand a language of despair.
But he already understands

so perhaps the pages will collect dog-ears and dust
among diasporas of Latin American dreams;
that he'll prefer to salsa on his rare
time off, maybe at the Cozumel on Tuesday nights,
with its specials on Cuervo and Corona,
and breathless partners spun into tops.

The Price of Labor

I. Obsolescence

A horseshoe tag stitched
above a Dickies back pocket
that once held daily wads of cash
and credit slips, now collects dust

and lint in the dim-lit basement,
their yoke and side seam having been sewn
together by deft brown hands, these pants
grown grayer than black.

When first bought, stiff enough for spills
to bead on the polyester blend, they relaxed
until all those washes grew cuffs
ragged and belt loops frayed.

I keep them shelved and folded neatly,
unsure of their uselessness.

II. Fatigue

The hard-plastic seats of the bus
are all I want but it never arrives.
My feet wet after work, cold midnight
seeps into every step of cracked soles.

The hard-plastic seats of the bus
don't hold me on the last turn one Friday.
I fall foolish on my back in the aisle
with a nearly empty bottle of pink wine.

The hard-plastic seats of the bus
are where young thugs grope my girl's ass.
Inert, I have no answer for their grabbing
hands when dared to do something about it.

It's like I'm a child
and all my bombs are water balloons.

Scraping Away

Once, when we were new, a plate of seafood
crashed to the kitchen tiles and became the first scallops
some of us had ever tried, scraping away
the broken to save the unscathed,

we chewed briny mouthfuls
of gritty sweet meat swimming
in a sniff of garlic and white wine, thinking
nothing ever tasted so good,

as that moment passed into sounds of clinking silverware
and carrying-on, while Perry Como sang overhead,
imploring us to learn the mambo's to and fro,
a lesson we'll soon take to humming

in a heaping world that needs us to believe
we can be oceans, pushing waves
toward a shoreline we can't see,
the worn down, far-off places of ourselves.

The World Feels Small after Shaking Hands with Bruno Sammartino

How comforting, Milgram's six degrees
of separation between any two people,
residents of a winding venue
in the widening web of our relations.

And on a slow night at the bistro, servers play
the Kevin Bacon Game for hours, connecting random celebs
to the onetime *Footloose* actor,
the center of the universe for those who dabble
in relative distance and fame.

I'll think of this as I shake hands
with the legendary pro wrestler I'm waiting on,
only two degrees from Schwarzenegger,
three from a Kennedy, five from
Alfred Hitchcock and Orson Welles.

And when the Irish writer tells me about showing
Arthur Miller the sights of Belfast, all I'm interested in
is this link to overdose and assassination. The closest I come
to conspiracy—a New Orleans barstool where Oswald once sat
and a shady landlord with mob ties.

Over the years, I've found myself sweating beside others
in hot restaurant kitchens. A few of them will succeed
at murder, suicide, or dying in their sleep.
A strange pride wells up when I come across
their names in the paper.

So, I stand two degrees from Jimmy Snuka,
three from Andy Warhol, four from Edward Teller,
and consider the misfortunes of some I've known—

the girl who jumped from a bridge,
the boy who died from a jealous lover's fire—

until I'm linked with a friend
who panhandles after losing his sight
to a mugger outside the 7-Eleven.
It feels like rubbernecking.

Party Girls

for Kathy, Ginny, and Nancy

By then, they'd thickened with middle age,
chugging up steps from the basement
Revel Room, working a wake or shower,
a retirement party where everything

was half-hearted and ending
with weak cocktails in small glasses,
the chafing dishes done burning
their Sterno, the hotel pans keeping

redskins and rigatoni warm enough
until those of us in the kitchen could clean up
the leftovers, all of us sweating
between shoulders, crabbing about tired legs,

wanting to wrap this shit up
before the shift even began.

The Corporate Fifty

for Dale

Nobody notices my two-syllable name
stamped on this thin brass rectangle,
tacked to a wooden plaque
near double doors that swing open then shut.
The red and white stripes of our uniforms
are the colors we bleed when cut. That was our joke.
You never notice a slice after it scars.
It is tough to be aware and live in skin.

My moniker lives in rows with eleven others awarded
the corporate fifty, names I helped pull out of the weeds,
then pounded beers with in back lots. Names
I had almost forgotten. Tonight, as I punch the clock,
the extra shifts leave me feeling shucked and exposed.
Tonight, faint praise is a destiny I don't recognize.

The Paper Signs

From the aqua vinyl booths
with touch table lamps to a motif
of clown collectibles, this restaurant
is kitsch and family relic in a franchised age.

Swinging wood doors
open into a kitchen
where paper signs remind us
of our status
as tipped employees.

Tacked on bulletin boards
like theories, they read:
No whining.
No smoking.
No reading the paper.
Keep your mouths shut
and do work.
Do not watch cooks.
Clean uniforms.
Coats downstairs.
Park in the upper lot.
If you don't
like rules, go down the road.

We bitch and grumble
when the boss posts
another missive.
Then we fold squares
of wine-colored cloth
into napkins and stack them
in milk crates like useful origami
creased by unacknowledged masters.

Demetrius's Glasses

All the girls on acid, sitting cross-legged on the carpet
of his unfurnished bedroom, would try them on,
thick lenses with brown plastic frames.
His glasses could amplify the best hallucinations.

Demetrius moved from the Y to sleep in a house of misfits
and stoners. Sometimes he would vanish. We all
feared daylight back then, not looking much beyond
months emptied of their useless laughter.

In those days, we looked shady dressed in yellow
Pasta Power T-shirts, busboys at Spaghetti Warehouse,
smoking joints in alleys between double shifts.
The passing dog walkers never said a word.

We haven't hung out for years. It's hard to know what to say
now that he's blind. I remember slipping on those glasses,
their magnified blur, remember feeling helpless, the way
he must feel, in the dark and without them now.

Cadre

On Fridays, I drive
a ginger-haired friend to work

another restaurant gig we landed
years before his first DUI,

and for ten minutes, we trade
tales of our aging parents,

their homes and bodies failing,
forgetting how they once told us

we could be anything, our promise
rusted as my red pickup that rumbles

into this back lot where air reeks
of grilled meat and dried sweat,

where busboys on break light
one stale smoke off another

and a cook rubs his last dime
over a stack of instant wins.

Tonight, what we've come to bear
beneath chandeliers built of driftwood

will be memories of those bad dreams,
their endless loads and slick floors

suffered until we wake,
bone-tired and thirsty.

Come midwinter, my weariness
a mouthful of *motherfucker*

spit when my truck gets trapped
in the driveway's icy grooves,

and like a child in tantrum,
all I can do

is rock my body
and spin the wheels into a cry.

Gratitude

Those first nights bussing tables
at the local red-sauce spot, I humped
greasy plates to the kitchen, and eyeballed
love-worn waitresses who paid me

no mind. It was the waiters
who made damn sure I moved with purpose,
setting the silverware straight, slicing
lemons into wedges with care.

In spotless oxfords and spit-shined shoes,
aprons cinched at the waist, they smoked
before the dinner rush, dishing out
tales of slinging drinks on the Vegas red-eye,

bragging about landing a double lutz
while skating Smurf-clad in the Ice Capades.
All of us, buzzing from laughter
by the time service began.

And even though the cooks joked
about them liking little boys
and holy rollers that year hyped
God's wrath for the coming plague,

those men tipped well and taught me
to fold napkins into swans, to powder
cornstarch on skin rubbed raw, to rescue
luster with a touch of vinegar, scrubbing

the parquet floors at shift's end
until my palms grew pickled.
They did it for this dipshit
who could down a dozen Stroh's

during a woodsy kegger, then gun
for cheap thrills, mocking, lisping
limp-wristed and swishy, as only
a straight kid from Pittsburgh could.

ii.

Memory is a physical thing made of proteins.
A cellular construction. A bridge over a chasm.

—Amy Wallen

Easy to Use as Modeling Clay

Elbow deep in the smells of grease
and rust, I'm stuffing the guts

of Grandpa's workbench
into a cardboard box—mismatched

nut and screw by the pound, a stray
doorknob from a Pittsburgh house,

those tiny bulbs for signal lights,
his car always a beater.

Tucked beneath one last shelf,
small jars of Plastic Steel nestled

in grimy cartons,
their black and gold script claiming

"a million uses" for just a buck.
Dried under each tin lid,

something leaden and gray
like what might've rested

at the bottom of this man I once adored,
a Hunky pipefitter known

to pack heat, to wear a wig
when stoned, to bully

when he didn't get his way.
I was six when he let me slug

his beer gut until my fist hurt.
Leaving the cellar, it's the dewy side

of his favorite glass I almost feel,
holding one hand against it,

skin and nail
helping him measure

two fingers of chilled vodka
until I could do it all on my own.

Last Offices

Fatty tumors bulging,
Mom's bluetick stumbles
up porch steps. She

was a pup when Dad landed
in long-term care, a vent pumping
all the breath he'd ever need.

Voice-robbed, he'd mouth *this sucks*
to any who'd ask, his body thinning
against sheets, trached and laid-up.

Mom, chattering, smooths
his greasy hair, helps him shave
before the nurses show

for what will be
his final sponge bath.
Fifteen years later, Mom's adding

cold bits of steak
to a tooth-marked bowl,
soaping paws and flanks

until the dog smells newborn
at this ending where the vet
lights a votive and a shot

renders fur quiet and still,
nose dry in which the scent
of my father is long dead.

My mother left
with only the sparking
memory of his touch.

Reason to Be

That lone brown bottle
of Dogfish Head left
in Mom's fridge
burdens us both,

so, when I stop by to spackle
and sand, declining
the beer and asking for water,
it lets our talk turn to Dad,

who, when he was living
always had a longneck handy,
damp circles marking
wherever he'd set them.

Humid June nights, he'd relax
on the front stoop, sweat beading
the once-chilly amber glass,
sticky paper labels growing soft.

Weekends, I'd ride unbelted
in his big blue Impala,
another uncapped Iron perched
in his lap as he'd drum

the dashboard with his fingers,
the radio cranking
with steady first notes
of "Shake, Rattle and Roll."

On the day's last stop
I'm left idling
in the ride as he'd belly up
to some bar, order a sixer

and one for the road, suds sticking
to his upper lip, while outside,
I grow restless knowing
Mom's city chicken is sizzling

even as the off-white Whirlpool,
with its Mr. Yuk magnet
and rusty metal shelves,
still needs to be replenished.

The Place Setting

Drunk the night before Grandpa's funeral,
I only half-remember throwing my father

against this cherrywood table
which has now been in my kitchen

for ten years, the crescent
under his left eye even longer.

It's a spindly sapling,
creaking and bending,

that neither breaks nor grows, gathering
time in its scratches and stains.

It's set the scene for beer-soaked tirades
those Sundays after work,

and the dinner parties we hold for two.
On it, three generations of women

have rolled *kluski,* powdering
pressed-out stretches with flour,

folding dough, then slicing out ringlets
before dropping them into bubbling water.

This slab has held
piles of folded boxers and socks,

pounds of pot, and blow scraped
into lines. Our slowly emptying red wines.

Candle wax being poured into molds.
The Crock-Pot's slow cooking.

A cell phone ringing,
telling me to visit Dad in ICU one last time.

Bully

Although it was my sister who took
the training wheels off my first bike,
and sex ed came from a spongy
copy of *Penthouse* stashed in the woods,

it was Dad who first taught me to ball a fist,
keep the thumb outside, and aim for the nose.
He wasn't thinking of the punches I'd later land
on Darrell's round head and Kool–Aid-stained mouth.

Year after year, I'd dish out the same pounding
each time he visited his aunt, our one-sided backyard
brawls becoming less about his weak Wiffle Ball play,
than my need for our game to end in his cries.

This is before I began to stare at the handicapped
or whipped Mom with a wire hanger, before I stoned stray cats,
and mistook cruelty for honesty when I asked my first
girlfriend if the rumors of her being a whore were true.

To say that I once preyed on the weak as if it were a rite
of passage would be to wonder if Darrell still remembers
how I taught him to spit blood, and swear at the top of his lungs,
learning at my hands how to give with all he had.

A Ginkgo Tree Teaches Me Something about Memory

Rooted to its sooty spit of land,
stony and still,
the ginkgo stands beside a boulevard
of whispering full-speed cars.
A living fossil shotgunning breath
through the wet-lipped world.

In class, I teach freshmen writers
the inanimate object
is a trigger to pull on the past,
to embrace detail
while they capture the dead
as a wedding band, a T-shirt,
or the smell of an aunt
whose cheap perfume
burned the throat,
their fingers trying to touch
all the ringed years under wrap.
One long dusty summer note.

Now, watching a season
change clothes
amid the falling rain,
I see how the ginkgo tree
drops its yellow leaves,
all at once, unlike our human loss
in sudden autumn.

The Toolbox

I search for the red-handled
Phillips-head among the clutter
of Dad's Air Force toolbox;
the obsolete, English-sized wrenches,
the vise-grips, and Channellocks looking
to grasp smooth-shouldered bolts
with their practical embrace.

The lesson I take from him:
find the proper tools for the job,
identify what works
from what is missing.
The screwdrivers we always lost.

I discovered freedom
in that basement at age twelve,
maintaining knobby
bike tires and caliper brakes,
sprocket and gooseneck,
stripping Allen keys and bruising
knuckles, learning
the words for failure and success.

His once-stenciled name
now faded to a smudge,
the smell of old grease mingling
with the leather decaying
on the useless handle.
Both artifact and history,
this metal rectangle could
just as easily hold his bones
beneath its lid and latch.

Sex Ed

A glossy scrap of mag caught in my hedge—
just an ad for makeup, but at first glance
it reminds me of the weathered *Penthouse*
I discovered at age twelve, stashed in the woods.

Bloated, spread open from the spine, left
near guzzled beer cans by older boys.
The centerfold page was Miss July 1984,
sticky from the damp and humid summer.

I squatted down in those flattened weeds
to thumb through picture spreads with fingers
nervous as the pulsebeat in my eardrums.
A rhythm built on equal parts, guilt and discovery.

All our fingerprints, on these softened papers
gritty with dirt. I let them dry and fade.

Napalm Summer

I make napalm all July
of that restless summer I turn fourteen,
after joyrides in Mom's Malibu
fail to hold their thrill,

after the redhead from up the street
invites some of us guys to watch porn
while she babysits,
and I'm the only one who shows.

So, when she hits *play* on the VCR,
I believe it's adulthood I'm entering
as the bathroom-stashed copy of *Taboo*
rolls over grainy tape heads to reveal

Oedipal overtones in a film where its stage-
named cast, with piston hips and bouncing breasts,
turn scenes of penetration into moments
that leave me dry-mouthed and breathless.

Flesh on flesh and throaty
animal moans fill the on-screen action,
but on the finer points
of passion and position,

I'm too callow to make a first move.
And having never kissed a girl yet,
nothing happens until I'm left with
a bike ride home and shorts full of throb.

The rest of that sticky month
I slice Dial soap into metal buckets of gasoline
that leave my basement reeking of fumes
as the mixture jellies beside the mower.

At dusk, I set fire to an open field,
try to turn desire into ash,
but melt the soles of my checkered Vans
trying to slow the lusty burn

down to a safe smolder where flames
flicker and tongue the dry grass,
like a want
needing to engulf me whole.

Slugger

On the narrow streets where I grow up
a southpaw wave or headlight flash
is all the harmony it takes
for drivers to settle right-of-way

until a traffic slight and a beer buzz
sets Dad off on a beeline to bash
our bald neighbor's head, spitting nails
and waving my dusty Louisville Slugger.

When Mom's cries won't turn him back
I'm sent to block the walkway,
a teen trying to pry
those thirty ounces of hard gray aluminum

from his machinist hands coiled
around its sticky black-taped handle.
This is the bat that smacked
a Little League triple.

Years later, a faded Ford blocking
my driveway for days
will set me off on a scramble
to its roof, trying to smash

this sedan as if it were a thousand empty cans,
a constellation of crescent dents left
before a window gets shattered,
my left hand bloodied.

And after a hazy morning of lying
to the cops, the heap gets towed,
bits of safety glass twinkling
my street for weeks,

the barest reminder of a feeling—
that summer fastball finding the sweet-
spotted barrel, my feet barely touching
ground as I rounded first base.

Fat Lady

The blows remind me of the repertoire of the schoolyard bully.
　　—William Gass

Severe as a noon siren,
her voice could slice
the neighborhood in two,

cutting through plaster walls
and shut windows, reminding
all of us within earshot

just how bad her kids could be.
Amid her fury, always a silent boyfriend
sitting tight, sucking at a Kool

on their crumbling stoop,
the screen door's slam punctuating
our long days that summer.

It was after the Fourth's grand finale,
when the dogs stopped panting
and pacing, and Dad had run out

of the M-80s he'd been tossing
at Mom's feet all day. His last longneck
uncapped, I break out my stash,

a gross of red-sticked bottle rockets
bank-rolled with paper route cash, the *fizz*
of each Zippo-lit wick followed

by the shrill whistle and *crack*
of gunpowder, leaving the air tangy
with sulfur as we start launching

dozens toward Fat Lady's
dingy green duplex nobody
ever rents for long.

Soon, she's waddling up the street,
two small boys in tow,
to stand with hands on hips

beneath a nearby streetlight, staring
our way as we grow quiet, hunkered
and sweating among the shadows.

Thirteen Steps

I.

For his last six years
my father geared each night
for the climb upstairs
by gulping swallows of air
into his shallow lungs.
The tether of oxygen
was necessary armor
against all thirteen steps,
against disappointment
that stretched to the edge
of his queen-size, now more
goal line than retreat.
Here he sat
with the clock radio
tuned to KDKA
and waited to see
if he would ever
get comfortable again.

II.

Each humid July
I hauled the air conditioner
up from the basement
to his window frame.
Under its awkward
weight I struggled
not to gouge plaster
divots from the walls,
its sharp-pointed metal

soon to be a humming box
of Emerson Quiet Kool.
My long feet plodded over
older-than-me burnt-orange carpet,
laid over joists
and squeaky floorboards.
This stairwell was once
my narrow playground,
a lumpy slide, a fort.
In recurrent dreams, I leap
from the top, weightless,
never reaching bottom.

What Dad Brought Home

The Swiss cuckoo clock, dark wood,
chirped out the hour just in time
to ruin the climax
of every Sunday Bond movie.

A box of Toblerone, triangular
chocolate with honey and nougat,
was a candy bar that no second-grader
in Pittsburgh should really like.

The souvenirs he brought home
live in memory alone: my favorite
yellow T-shirt with Iowa outlined
in black and a single stalk of corn.

Mom pronounced it "I-OWE-ER."
Her English was a second language
she rarely butchered except this one
word, a state strange with accent.

Limited to a ten-mile radius
for his last decade, it was easy to forget
that Dad used to travel for his job,
radial riveter service technician,

that they met in the Air Force,
that once he was young, and
that she was from Maine
and even younger.

Wrist Rocket

Taking aim one-eyed
while the other stays shut,
I peer between prongs
of a borrowed slingshot and think

their crux makes a peace sign.
The elastic violence begins
as I stretch the band
of rubber tubing to behind my right ear,

a stone missile hugged
in a leather pouch, pinched
between a trinity of fingers.
I stand at the core of potential energy,

after school at age twelve,
feet crunching leaves,
unsure of how
this is going to end.

Some days we gather ammo,
iron ore pellets that fall from coke cars
piled high and headed down to the ovens.
They scatter between the heavy gray railroad stones.

One day the dads get laid off
and industry begins to go away slowly.
Abandoned rails and mills,
pulled up deep-rooted weeds.

A town's decay that begins
like the cries of the wounded, then stiffens
with rigor beneath the skin.
Rust on my hands, I let that shot fly.

*I knew the way music can fill a room,
even with loneliness, which is of course
a kind of company.*

—William Matthews

Impermanence

Outside that rusty warehouse in Warren, PA,
tall grass scattered with litter
waits to be whacked, while close-by,
plastic chairs circle a dusty table
where no one gripes about their hours
during smoke breaks anymore.

Inside these gray spaces commerce forgot,
silence rubs itself raw
among corners where shadows fall
and take years to fade.
I look for my image, refracted
in the jagged remains
of a hundred cracked panes that, even as a kid,
I knew would've been shameful to stone.

Iron City Sage

No one from the Eagle's Club showed
for his funeral, and it took eight years for my father
to step into my dreams, looking hungry and disheveled
as on those Sunday mornings I scrambled us eggs and burned bacon.

From his weekend easy chair, he'd study world war,
a Parliament smoldering in that metal ashtray
my sister bought him a decade before he winded easily.
By night, with the Iron's going down easy, he'd forget to eat

then start with his playful jabs, asking me
how tall I was, and with my answer he'd reply
he didn't know they piled shit that high. I'd chuckle,
playing the faithful drinking buddy I couldn't be at fifteen.

It took me until his end, when those blue tubes moved air
through his ruined lungs, to appreciate
how he shared himself through scraps and tales,
the sum of his wisdom coming when he said,

this world doesn't need any more assholes.
Sometimes, after the bar, he'd stand in our kitchen
to conduct an invisible orchestra, arms waving
while a cassette did its best to squeeze

each blissful note of Beethoven's Sixth
through a tinny boom box. At the movement's finale,
he'd puff another smoke then turn to remind me
to always strive for greatness, a raw-boned man

in jeans and untucked work shirt, hoping
to make my heart and mind simmer
before he chased down each of his whims
with a gulp of beer.

Initiation

State College, 1993

After backpacking
a skunky brick of Mexican
on a long bus ride, the best
Happy Valley has to offer
is a love seat,

some piss-warm Pabst,
and a gray moray gliding
through a filthy tank
while dusty speakers spill
Bitches Brew,

its low end grooves
haunting every inch
of this dank room, shuttered
from the coming
fall morning.

Across another lost weekend
those scuffed discs
purists love to hate
keep spinning—
their binge-worthy vamp

keyed to drone and slither,
a table set
for Miles to tap
spines with blasting
echoed notes, electric

pickups clipped
to his muted bell

where a full breath can stir
sounds, dark and ominous
to my untrained ears.

Section 620

June 30, 1995

From the upper decks of Three Rivers, poured
onto Pittsburgh's North Side as a multiuse stadium,
circa 1970, a place with all the character of a concrete ashtray,
imploded since we swayed

that night away, thousands deep in the psychedelic darkness,
moving among steep aisles and plastic yellow seats,
lit and spun on LSD and K while the Dead played,
unknown to us all, one of their final shows,
before Jerry Garcia could no longer rise to play
another encore,
and I forgot I was afraid of heights.

Rain played metaphor
as the second set began, the muggy air wet
with synchronicity and improvisation. We stayed
dry under an overhanging roof and chewed on ice cubes,
knowing convergence is something to behold,
the sizzle of good vibes coming together amid Astroturf
and summer storm. Here, there was no Ginsberg or Kesey,
and I would never whirl like a dervish, trying hard to hold
my head on straight, wishing earlier that blue June day,
among the asphalt parking lots, among the beer bottles,

for the hunger of a constant moon,
one that could hover
and hold still time
before places and days like these are all gone.

Bebop Alarm Clock

Inside a small rectangle
of black plastic and red-eyed numbers
was a tuning bar
sometimes too broad to find
the decimals of narrow bandwidth.
A jazz station tucked between static
on the clock radio tuner's two-way street.

A single speaker stuck beneath a ridged grille
could pucker a brain with blood,
collect from those midnight-blue heavens
all the desire and sadness in the world,
make heart, lungs syncopate and praise
madmen musicians who wrung out of this wrong century
something alive and escaped.

Two-Drink Minimum

When John T. shotgunned joint-smoke past my lips
    at the party where everyone spoke at once, not eating
a thing, it was green of me to not think I'd been kissed.
    His last name's gone to me now,
even as I first met him—on his back, spitting

through his mustache, twitching on the tan-tiled kitchen floor—
    my first days wearing
red and white stripes, suspenders not yet decked with flair-pins.
    His black cap lying
crumpled and tossed aside while burgers went cold and the fryer
    kept sizzling away.

At Golden Lantern, weeks later, John T. tells me
    he's a laid-off autoworker from Flint.
He goes by Alice, a nickname Lucille, the bald barkeep, gave him
    in this gay bar that sounds like a dance party
and never closes. A place where a sobriety token can buy you
    a rum & Coke.

And I know I'm far from Pittsburgh when, days after, on my way
    down Royal Street, I'll find him snoring
in a doorway. Thin, pink-faced, and goggle-eyed, he weaves
    his way to work, a place he calls
a two-drink minimum—that being what it takes to get him
    through the heavy double doors.

At forty-something, his body's a hollowed-out haywire
    of epilepsy and HIV. When he cleans out
the book bag he calls home, a dozen empty Gilbey's pints clink inside.
    When he refuses the meds, he blames them
for shitting himself on the Uptown streetcar one night.

I forget now the lies I told myself about what I was doing
    for that year in the Quarter,
but mostly, I listened to denial as it gathered
    in a pool of sweat beneath
melted cocktails, headwater to the tiny rivers we floated upon.

"Do You Know What It Means to Miss New Orleans?"

—Kermit Ruffins, Live at Vaughan's

By the time that plate shatters
its jagged slice from my hand
and medics kick apart
our rotted French doors

hoping they can staunch
the flow before rolling us
red-lit and howling
across Canal Street,

we'll find our days
numbered in this city
gritty with want, blaming
the hooch and *yayo*

for leaving us raw-scraped
and licking our lips numb
as another dawn inches
its way over.

It was something to first feel
the way heat climbs
into every fold here,
the pavement sizzling

while a sax-man sweats
through another sugary cover,
busking on sidewalks
hosed-down each morning

after being painted
by tourists ripped
from the potent rum slush
plied on every corner.

When we skip town,
all we leave of ourselves
adds up to Carnival beads
and bloodstains, an unpaid lease,

that neighbor's Hoover
we borrowed, then broke,
and in the Quarter's wet cement,
our initials still drying.

Additional Parking for Big Pete's Blues Wagon

In the glide-by scenery of June,
one steel sign hangs,

to a heavy sag of chain
stretched across cement-stuffed posts,

its seven purple words glistening
with windblown mist.

Stuck on this drizzly drive
down Route 3, with only pop and talk

on the rental's radio,
I glance at a place where summer

trees once danced and swayed
before the crowds gave out.

Here, bands rode twanging
Delta grooves, gutbucket and gospel

into the call-and-response of soulful release,
buckling hearts, rattling windows.

Later on, blue notes would steam
from a boss horn's bottomless bell

until the walls flaked mojo, and left
memories, now curled yellow,

fingers keeping time, tapping
a night away on wobbly, beer-sticky tables.

Big Pete's

locked doors and gravel lot,
wrung dry of its music.

"You Can't Be in Heaven and on Earth at the Same Time"

was how Sonny Rollins once described
woodshedding on the Williamsburg,
neighborly complaints
leading him to practice
on the bridge's deck, stretching
his breath at all hours

until sturdy notes took bloom,
strident enough to serenade
cars changing lanes, the honking
seasons turning his stage hiatus
into years of playing
for many-weathered skies.

Arriving on the heels of Ornette's
new sound, Rollins declared
his return with *The Bridge*,
the last cassette I'd buy
before dropping
out of college,

its "God Bless the Child,"
never failing to cue
an image of my skinny pal,
Stoner Bob, camped
below that underpass,
near the jail,

his rocky nook bearing
tents, torn sleeping bags,
and the tags of local

Wild Style legends, their bent
yard-high script reading
like a code of Krylon pastels.

Then last week, a ragtag
drumline jamming
under a yellow span had me
longing for the impossible—
a brass winged solo calling out,
far above us all.

Grasping

I.

All those good times
might've been what Duke
had in mind when vamping

his silky-fingered B-flats,
letting Coltrane counter
until tenor notes cluster

close to the bone, their take
on "In a Sentimental Mood"
leaving me grasping at our dreamy past,

where each New Orleans morning,
having snorted our way
through another cocaine night,

we lovers wait on Valium's coldcock
in our digs above that drag-
queen bar near the Quarter's edge.

II.

Lately, my neck tingles
hearing Sarah Vaughan honey
the hi-fi, bending Duke's tune

around Mundell Lowe's crisp
guitar lines until the melody
makes me wistful for how we'd stagger

just before dawn, so eager to find
a pocket of deep sleep
among the disco bumping below,

our darkened bedroom glowing
with sitcoms snagged
by rabbit ears, the roaches

clicking behind walls
while canned laughter ran
over our thinning listless bodies.

Caravan

for Nathan Davis

Before we chugged
those jugs of Ruby Red,
before I moved to New Orleans
and got shacked up
across from Congo Square,

before we dropped bombs
on the tom and snare
of a busted trap set
that once littered
his dust-webbed basement,

Mick and I'd blow off
jive-ass jobs to bang out
big beats on Schenley Park's
fallen trees, pounding
broken oak branches

on weathered trunks, aping
Blakey chopping wood
on thundering cuts we first heard
in a class led
by Dolphy's last tenor man.

And when the lights rimming
the hollow began to buzz,
it was enough to share a smoke
and let our sweat cool
before we'd wrap.

Punk

I keep embarrassment in a stash,
stacked and piled like yellowed news
in cracked plaster rooms,
off behind the kitchen table of my mind,

a place to visit my drunken faux pas,
file away the fuckups, and feel bad
about the time I hit an old woman in the mouth
with a jar full of maraschino cherries.

Sometimes, I thumb through to that time
when Leo and I were sixteen,
and we sat parked for hours
in front of the Electric Banana,

a punk club we'll never go inside
out of fear our night might end
in a busted nose from a swirling
mosh pit full of knees.

Our missed chance to stomp
and bleed on a sticky dance floor
still jangles like loose change in a pocketful
of sad attempts to fit in.

But, it's only after Leo's blond hair is lost to glue
and malt liquor in a botched attempt at dreadlocks,
after he buzzed it close to the skull and we lose touch,
that I'll come to know so well those

Minor Threat cassettes that click
in a dusty Delco tape deck while we watch
the Iron City punks loiter about the Banana's front door
in their comfortable Mohawks and effortless combat boots.

Marooned and sober behind
a foggy windshield,
a lush hillside
fails to take shape,

and I find that, decades later,
I am a self full of deeds undone, going places
where so much is an idling Chevy
with a paint job the color of contusion.

The Communicants

Here, Tuesday stumbling
toward midnight, we're stuck

with that lone couple lingering
over a last swallow of Pinot,

their plates cleared, water glasses
emptied, check unsettled.

They don't care
that the closing cook has swept

and mopped his now-dark kitchen
where the dish machine cools

among bottles of bleach,
or that last call was given long ago.

Instead, they lean in and whisper
while we sip water

and try not to stare, soaking up
the flicker of a muted TV,

feeling forgotten
like those doggie bags we pack

that get left behind. And if work
can be worship, it finds us

supplicant and waiting
for the chirp of chairs pushing

back from their table, followed
by heels clicking on hardwood,

a recessional marking
the end of service, the front door

closing like a prayer,
quiet on its hinges.

ACKNOWLEDGMENTS

Much gratitude goes out to the editors of the following publications for publishing my work:

5AM: "Demetrius's Glasses"
Briar Cliff Review: "Additional Parking for Big Pete's Blues Wagon"
Brilliant Corners: "Caravan" and "Initiation"
Burlesque Press: "A Ginkgo Tree Teaches Me Something about Memory"
Floodwall Magazine: "Punk"
The Fourth River: "'Do You Know What It Means to Miss New Orleans?'" and "Reason to Be"
Jerry Jazz Musician: "Grasping"
Mason's Road: "José at the Yum-Yum Café"
Nerve Cowboy: "Bebop Alarm Clock," "Napalm Summer," "Sex Ed," and "Two-Drink Minimum"
Open: Journal of Arts & Letters: "Fat Lady," "Party Girls," and "The World Feels Small after Shaking Hands with Bruno Sammartino"
Paterson Literary Review: "Iron City Sage"
Pittsburgh City Paper's Chapter & Verse section: "Curse" and "Wrist Rocket"
Pittsburgh Poetry Review: "Slugger"
Pittsburgh Post-Gazette: "The Corporate Fifty," "The Paper Signs," "Thirteen Steps," "What Dad Brought Home"
Poet Lore: "Impermanence," "Scraping Away," and "'You Can't Be in Heaven and on Earth at the Same Time'"

Review Americana: "The Communicants"
Shaking Like a Mountain: "Section 620"
SLAB: "Argot"
Spry: "Bully"
The Sow's Ear: "Gratitude"
Third Wednesday: "Cadre" and "Easy to Use as Modeling Clay"
Vox Populi: "The Toolbox"

"Argot" is featured in the documentary *Eating & Working & Eating & Working* by filmmaker David Bernabo. The film focuses on the lives of local service-industry workers.

"The Paper Signs" also appears in the anthology *Verse Envisioned* (Word Association Publishers, 2016).

"Scraping Away" was a 2017 selection for the Pennsylvania Public Poetry Project.

CAVANKERRY'S MISSION

CavanKerry is committed to expanding the reach of poetry and other fine literature to a general readership by publishing works that explore the emotional and psychological landscapes of everyday life and relationships.

OTHER BOOKS IN THE EMERGING VOICES SERIES

Printing this book on 30-percent PCW and FSS-certified paper saved 2 trees, 1 million BTUs of energy, 127 pounds of CO_2, 67 pounds of solid waste, and 524 gallons of water.

Scraping Away has been set in Acumin Pro, a neo-grotesque sans-serif typeface, intended for a balanced and rational quality. It was designed by Robert Slimbach for Adobe in 2015.